MILFORD HAVEN WATERWAY

Brian John

Pembrokeshire Coast National Park

Area Guide

1981

CONTENTS

INTRODUCTION

Milford Haven is one of the finest natural harbours in the world. It extends from the south-west coast of Dyfed right into the heart of the old county of Pembroke, carrying tidal waters as far inland as Haverfordwest on the Western Cleddau and Canaston Bridge on the Eastern Cleddau. The waterway is over 18 miles (29 km) long. At its mouth the Haven is 1¼ miles (2 km) wide, and it is still over half a mile wide as far inland as Pembroke Dock. In this outer section of the waterway the main channel has at least 50 ft (15 m) of water even at low tide, although mud flats are exposed in shallow embayments such as Angle Bay and the Pembroke River. About 9½ miles (15 km) inland the estuary has a north-south alignment, and the character of the waterway changes dramatically above Neyland and Burton; upstream from here, the Daugleddau is a sheltered tidal estuary with steep wooded sides and

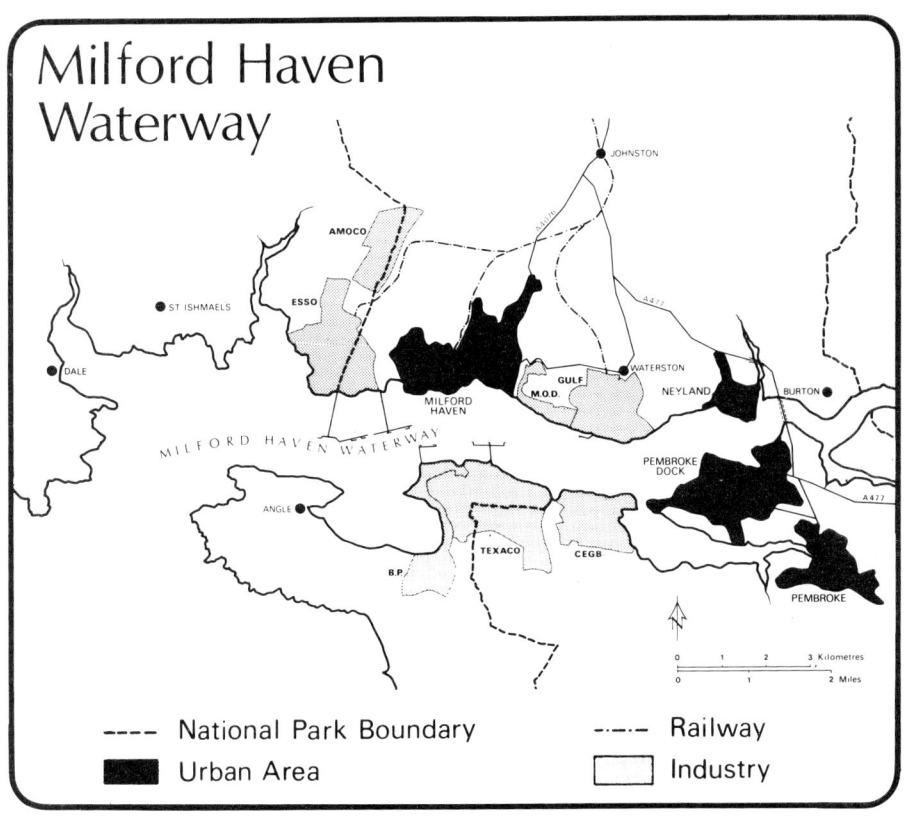

Map of Milford Haven Waterway, showing main towns and industrial sites.

with many small inlets and branches which are locally referred to as "pills".

This booklet is concerned with the Milford Haven waterway proper, i.e. the section which can be used by large ships at all states of the tide. It extends from St. Ann's Head as far inland as Burton and the Milford Haven Bridge, and it includes on both shores sections of the Pembrokeshire Coast National Park. The middle reaches of the waterway, which are for the most part outside the Park boundary, include the towns of Milford, Neyland, Pembroke Dock and Pembroke. This section has been transformed within the last 20 years by the oil industry, and it now supports one of Europe's largest oil-refining complexes. Milford Haven is, however, much more than an oil port, and it is the purpose of this booklet to describe the environment, the history and the main man-made features of this fascinating area.

The Daugleddau section of the waterway is not described here in any detail. This very beautiful and remote district is designated as a separate 'sector' of the National Park, and in view of its unique scenery and distinctive industrial and trading history it is dealt with in a separate Area Guide.

THE ORIGINS OF THE HAVEN

The deep, ancient river valley which has been flooded by the sea to form Milford Haven is aligned approximately east-west. This conforms with the structures (such as folds and faults) created during the Armorican mountain-building episode which affected west Wales about 300 million years ago. The main channel of Milford Haven has been eroded along a faulted line of weakness in the rocks, and in particular along an outcrop of Carboniferous Limestone. This rock, which is soluble in water, has also been eroded away to form some of the embayments on the Haven's south shore. From the geological map we can see how narrow outcrops of Carboniferous Limestone have been etched out during millions of years of river and coastal erosion to form the inlets of West Angle Bay, Angle Bay, Pembroke River and Cosheston Pill.

Milford Haven was probably formed more than two million years ago. Originally it must have been a broad river valley occupied by a slow meandering stream which reached the sea some way to the west of the present coastline. Sea-level at this time was at least 100 ft (30 m) lower than at present. With the onset of the Ice Age the climate cooled drastically, and on at least two occasions the gigantic Irish Sea Glacier, flowing south-eastwards from St. George's Channel, over-rode the coasts of the Haven. The ice itself did not have a great effect upon the local scenery,

4

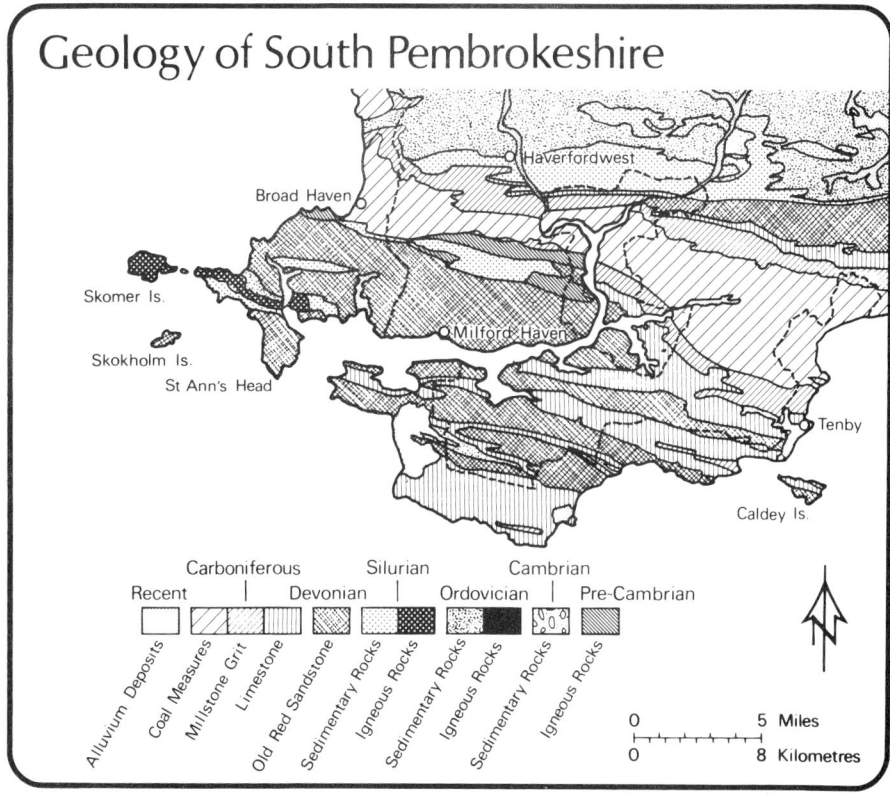

Geology of South Pembrokeshire

Haverfordwest

Broad Haven

Skomer Is.

Skokholm Is.

St Ann's Head

Milford Haven

Tenby

Caldey Is.

Carboniferous | Silurian | Cambrian
Recent | Devonian | Ordovician | Pre-Cambrian

Alluvium Deposits | Coal Measures | Millstone Grit | Limestone | Old Red Sandstone | Sedimentary Rocks | Igneous Rocks | Sedimentary Rocks | Igneous Rocks | Sedimentary Rocks | Igneous Rocks

0   5 Miles
0   8 Kilometres

Geological map of Milford Haven and South Pembrokeshire, showing how the outlines of the waterway are influenced by rock type.

but at the end of each glacial episode large volumes of water were released by the melting ice. Meltwater torrents deepened the old river valley and also cut new channels around the entrance of the Haven. At Mullock Bridge (SM 811078), near Dale, a broad *Kame terrace* of sand and gravel was deposited by meltwater streams flowing along the edge of a mass of decaying glacier ice. Now it has been almost entirely removed through gravel-working.

Sea-levels remained low during the glacial episodes of the Ice Age, but during the *interglacials* the sea flooded into Milford Haven. On at

least one occasion it rose to a higher level than at present, creating cliffs and narrow rock-cut benches along both shores. Today the valley is flooded by the sea again, and the Haven is considered a classic example of a *ria*[1].

At the present day the shores of the waterway are being altered above all else by marine processes. However,

---

[1]A *ria* is a river-eroded valley flooded by a rise of sea level. A *fjord,* on the other hand, is cut by glacial erosion and flooded by the sea following the retreat of glacier ice.

5

Bedded sands and gravels at Mullock Bridge, near Dale. These deposits were laid down in a kame terrace by glacial meltwater.

wave-action is by no means as effective as on the outer coasts of Pembrokeshire, for the southward-projecting Dale Peninsula acts as a barrier to much of the oceanic swell approaching from the west. The tidal mud-flats of Angle Bay and the Pembroke River support salt-marsh vegetation and are indicative of relatively still-water conditions. The Haven proper has a tidal range of up to 26 ft (8 m), and tidal currents scour the main channel and prevent a build-up of the alluvial silt and clay carried seawards by the two Cleddau rivers.

The local climate is relatively mild. St. Ann's Head, at the mouth of Milford Haven, has an average daily mean temperature for January of about 6.2°C (43°F), while the average daily mean for July is 15.3°C (60°F), these figures indicate a remarkably small annual temperature range. All the shores of the Haven receive less than 40" (100 cm) of rainfall per year, and snow is a rarity. Strong winds are common, especially from the west and south-west, and the many frontal depressions which pass across the area give rise to rapid weather changes. Sunshine totals are over 1500 hours per year, and compared with almost all other ports in the U.K. Milford Haven experiences remarkably little fog.

EARLY SETTLEMENT

The Stone Age

The earliest settlement traces in Milford Haven date from the Old Stone Age or Palaeolithic period. About 18,000 years ago, when most of Britain was held in the grip of glacial ice, the Southern margin of the Irish Sea Glacier lay in the vicinity of Milford Haven. Sea-level was more than 330 ft (100 m) lower than it is now; the coastline lay far to the west and the floor of the Haven was occupied by torrential meltwater streams, areas of barren frozen ground and patches of marshy tundra. Among the wild animals which roamed this broad valley were Mammoth, Giant Deer, Woolly Rhinoceros, Cave Bear, Cave Lion,

Wolf and Reindeer. Small family groups of hunters lived in caves such as the Priory Farm Cave at Monkton (SM 978018), leaving behind them traces of intermittent occupation over thousands of years. Later on, during the Mesolithic period, the climate improved and thick forest spread over the floor and sides of Milford Haven. Hunting and fishing people ranged over the area, sometimes living in caves and sometimes in primitive shelters near the lagoons and rivers which provided much of their food-supply. As the climate warmed sea-level rose, eventually flooding into the Haven and submerging peatlands, marshes and woodlands. At the same time many of the traces of Mesolithic settlement were lost.

About 5,000 years ago the first waves of Neolithic settlers arrived in the area. They were farmers, and they began to alter the landscape through shifting cultivation and the selective burning and felling of the forest. They also kept domesticated animals, and herds of cattle prevented 'natural' forest regeneration in many areas through their grazing habits and their liking for succulent tree saplings. The Neolithic settlers had quite sophisticated religious rituals, and a number of their burial chambers or *cromlechs* have been found in the Milford Haven area, for example Devil's Quoit, on Kilpaison Burrows (SM 886008). The immigrants retained many trading links (by land and sea) with other areas around St. George's Channel.

The Age of Metal

By about 3,500 years ago the Neolithic and Mesolithic peoples who lived together in South Pembrokeshire had been joined by Bronze Age peoples. Among the main traces left

in the landscape from this period are the round barrows on the line of the ancient Ridgeway between Penally and Pembroke and to the south of the Haven, and the standing stones near Sandy Haven. During the Iron Age (which began about 2,500 years ago) there was a great immigration of Celtic peoples. Most of them arrived by sea, and from their abundant earthworks (mostly defended settlements known as 'hill forts' or 'promontory forts') we know that they took over the whole of Pembrokeshire. There must have been a long period of tribal conflict before the territory of the *Demetae* (as they were known in Roman times) began to be secure.

Left: Iron Age hill fort at Merrion - one of the few well-preserved ancient earthworks in the Milford Haven area.

Romans, Celts and Vikings

During the centuries which followed the birth of Christ the Milford Haven waterway was used by many different peoples. The Romans had very little impact upon the far west of Wales, but during the early centuries of the Christian Era Pembrokeshire became one of the centres of Celtic culture. Milford Haven figured prominently in the great folk migrations which linked Wales and Ireland. By the middle of the sixth century the kingdom of Dyfed was established, and for several centuries after this there was a great deal of missionary activity in the Milford Haven area as elsewhere in Pembrokeshire. This period, often referred to as the Age of the Saints, gave Wales its Christianity, its language and its culture.

In the tenth and eleventh centuries the Vikings became frequent visitors to Milford Haven and the adjacent coasts. Usually they came on raiding or trading expeditions, and the waterway (which must have reminded the Norsemen of the deep sheltered fjords of southern and western Norway) was probably often used as a supply and repair base. There is a tradition that a chieftain called Hubba wintered in the Haven with a fleet of 23 ships and 2,000 men, and Milford Haven may even have become the centre of a Viking settlement. No direct evidence for this has ever been found, but names like Dale, Hubberston, Musselwick, Hasguard, and Gelliswick survive to show us that Norse language and culture must have made quite an impact, at least upon the inhabitants of the outer reaches of the waterway. The earliest references to Milford itself (e.g. in 1207) are to Mellferth, a Norse form meaning a fjord with sandbanks. "Haven" is a later addition.

Milford Haven Waterway - a seafaring centre since Viking times.

MILFORD HAVEN AND LITTLE ENGLAND

Conquest and Settlement

In 1093 the Norman conquest of Pembrokeshire began, and as the armies of Roger of Montgomery and other adventurers annexed the old Welsh territories the Milford Haven waterway became immensely important from a strategic point of view. The Normans and their Anglo-Saxon followers overran South Pembrokeshire within a few years, and they immediately began to put down roots. In the Milford Haven area earthworks were put up at St. Ishmael's, Walwyn's Castle and Castlemartin; and later on stone castles were built at Dale and Pembroke. The castle at Pembroke (SM 982016), originally a motte, was enlarged and elaborated in the thirteenth century to become the most formidable of all the stone fortresses of Pembrokeshire. At the same time the town of Pembroke grew to the east of the castle, strung out along a limestone ridge and protected by its town walls. Each castle became a focus for Anglo-Norman settlement, and during the early decades of Little England's history many completely new villages were built on both sides of the waterway. Some of these were not located in fortified sites at all. The villages were populated partly by the original Welsh inhabitants of the area, but as the 'new' landscape of the Englishry evolved thousands of immigrants were brought in from Devon and Cornwall, Somerset and Gloucester and even further afield. The names on the parish map of

Pembroke Castle - the Great Keep. It dates from about 1200, and is among the finest in the British Isles.

South Pembrokeshire show just how anglicised the area became. In the twelfth century at least three waves of Flemish immigrants were brought in to Milford Haven to strengthen the colony in the face of continuing resistance from the dispossessed Welsh princes. Some of the Flemings were settled in the *cantref* of Rhos, on the north shore of the waterway, thus adding further spice to the mix of peoples living in the area.

9

The Later Middle Ages

The waterway of Milford Haven played a crucial part in the founding and consolidation of Little England. The Welsh were not great seafarers, and no doubt the waterway was used over and again for the supply and relief of the garrisons and immigrant communities at Pembroke and other places further inland. The Haven's sheltered waters were used by Henry II for the assembly of the fleet which was dispatched for the conquest of Ireland. Later on, in 1405, a French army came by sea to Milford Haven with the objective of helping Owain Glyndwr in his revolt against the English Crown. After spending the winter of 1405-06 in the area they left again, having achieved precisely nothing.

Perhaps the most famous event in the history of Milford Haven was the landing near Dale by Henry Tudor and his forces on 7th August, 1485.

Henry, who had been born at Pembroke Castle in 1457, was here among his own people. A product of Little England, he was nevertheless of Welsh royal descent. Welsh people had, during the young man's exile in France, come to identify their aspirations for self-respect and self-determination with his aspirations for the English crown. After his triumphant landing Henry gained the allegiance of many of the forces of south Pembrokeshire. He marched through Haverfordwest and Newport to Cardigan, and thence to Machynlleth, gathering the support of many Welsh-speaking troops on the way. At the Battle of Bosworth he defeated the army of Richard III. Richard himself was slain on the battlefield, and in the person of Henry VII the Tudor dynasty ascended the English throne.

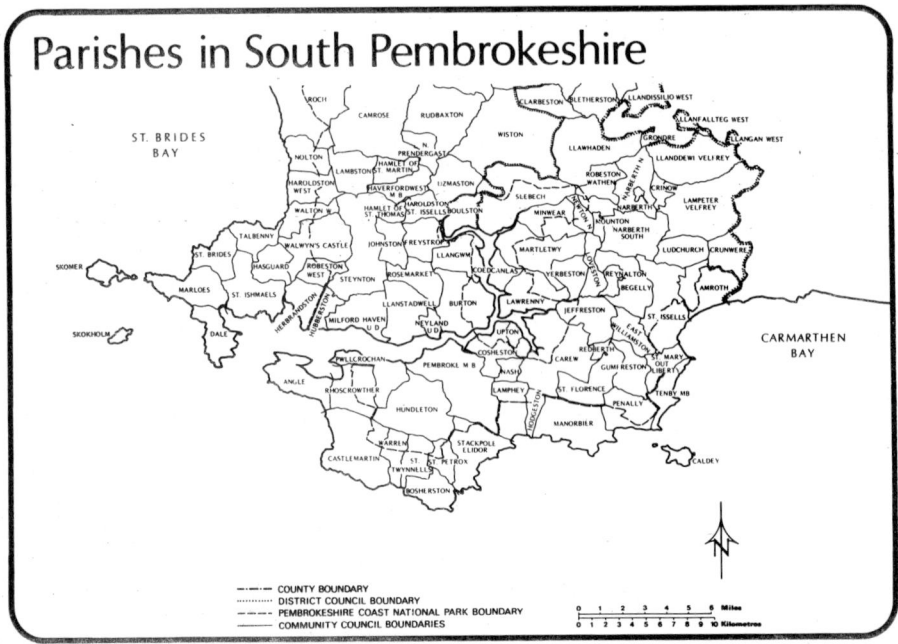

Parishes in South Pembrokeshire

10

SEA TRADING

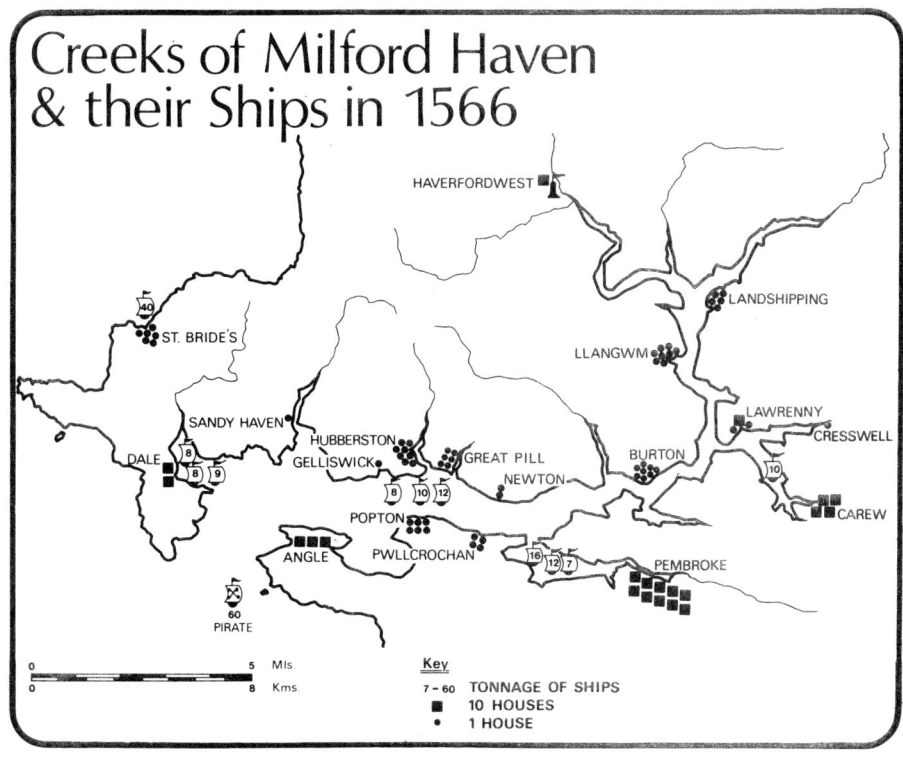

Creeks of Milford Haven & their Ships in 1566

HAVERFORDWEST

LANDSHIPPING

ST. BRIDE'S 40

LLANGWM

LAWRENNY
CRESSWELL

SANDY HAVEN
HUBBERSTON
GELLISWICK
GREAT PILL
BURTON
DALE 8
NEWTON
8 9
8 10 12
10
CAREW

POPTON
ANGLE PWLLCROCHAN
16 12 7
PEMBROKE

PIRATE 60

```
0        5  Mls
0        8  Kms
```

Key

7 – 60 TONNAGE OF SHIPS
■ 10 HOUSES
• 1 HOUSE

Map showing the main trading centres of the waterway in 1566.

With the advent of more peaceful times following the Act of Union of 1536 the seaborne trade of South Pembrokeshire increased steadily. By this time the rich farming lands around Milford Haven were thickly peopled and productive, with sizeable agricultural surpluses. In the Middle Ages there had been many trading

---

Left: Parish map of South Pembrokeshire. The parish names show how anglicised the area had become by the Later Middle Ages.

links with Ireland, France and the Bristol Channel towns, and in the sixteenth century Pembroke and Haverfordwest developed into important ports with well-stocked warehouses, thriving markets and wealthy merchant classes. Most of the sailing ships recorded in the port books were small coasters of under 20 tons. They brought in household goods, hardware or clothing from Bristol, wine and salt from France, timber, hops, pitch, dried and fresh fruit, and spices and other exotic goods from Spain and Portugal. Among the most important exports were grain, cattle, hides and skins, wool, coal and culm, and barrels of salt herring. There was also a considerable trade in limestone, burnt in coastal lime kilns and used as an essential dressing for the land all over Pembrokeshire. On the shores of Milford Haven the main centre of sea trading was the old town of Pembroke, but Dale and Angle were busy small ports, and sailing vessels also called regularly at Popton, Pwllcrochan, Hubberston and Great Pill. All of these localities enjoyed the advantages of sheltered beaches and a large tidal range, so local people were spared the need to build elaborate harbours or breakwaters. Here and there stone quays or wooden jetties were built, but most of these were in the muddy creeks of the Daugleddau; in the outer reaches of the waterway small sailing vessels were generally loaded and unloaded at low tide on sandy or stony beaches.

Shipbuilding

There was a busy shipbuilding industry in Milford Haven during Elizabethan times, and the construction of sailing vessels continued almost till the end of the nineteenth century. On the shores of the waterway there were no proper shipyards: shipwrights used temporary slipways on suitable beaches, building their vessels just above high water mark. They used local oak and some imported timbers, and sails, fittings and ropes were generally made by local craftsmen. Ketches and sloops of less than 20 tons and under 40 feet (12 m) long were generally built within the space of a year, with teams of 15-30 men involved in the construction. In the later 1700s, and in the 1800s, larger sloops of 20-40 tons were built, as well as schooners and square-rigged vessels of 100 tons or more.

An old hulk rotting in the mud of Angle Bay.

Smuggling and Piracy

During Tudor and Stuart times smuggling and piracy were commonplace in Pembrokeshire waters, and inevitably Milford Haven became something of a focus for illegal seaborne activities. Pembroke and Haverfordwest were openly visited by vessels whose masters sold off duty-free goods, and the trading activities of smugglers and pirates were quite often aided and abetted by respectable merchants, local municipal officials, or even magistrates. Some of the creeks or pills of Milford Haven were used by smugglers who appeared out of the blue, found a ready local market for their goods, and then quietly disappeared out to sea. In this far western corner of the realm it was none too easy for customs men and other officials to keep a regular check on all the possible landing places of the waterway.

FORTIFICATIONS

The Norman adventurers who conquered most of Pembrokeshire and created Little England Beyond Wales were in no doubt about the strategic importance of Milford Haven. It acted as a lifeline in the many conflicts with the Welsh princes during the colony's first three centuries, and the Anglo-Norman defence system depended upon the control of the waterway which penetrated into the very heart of the colonial lands. The early Norman motte and bailey structures, and later the stone castles, show a distinct preference for easily defended bluffs overlooking tidal water. Later on, during the Civil War, the Parliamentary fleet controlled the waters of the Haven, relieved the beleaguered garrison in Pembroke Castle, and was able to support various land operations by transporting troops, food supplies and armaments. This maritime superiority was crucial for the Parliamentary cause; without it the course of the Civil War in Wales would have been quite different.

Surprisingly, the Milford Haven waterway was not properly protected by fortifications until the middle of the nineteenth century. As early as 1539 Thomas Cromwell had stressed the need for surveys and fortifications, and in 1580 Henry VIII embarked on an ambitious plan to fortify both shores. Two blockhouses were built on the north and south sides of the Haven entrance, but they seem never to have been effectively maintained and in the absence of any strategic threat to the western seaboard of Wales no further works were undertaken.

By about 1840 considerable changes had occurred both in European politics and in the development of the Haven. The new town of Milford had been built on the

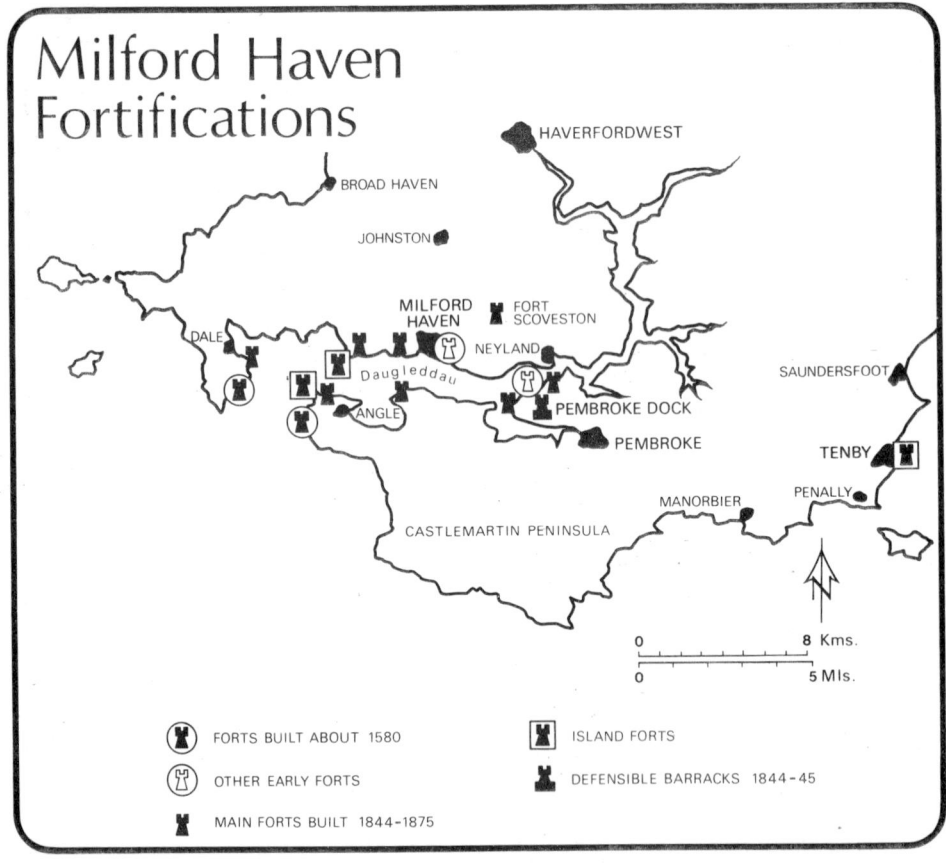

Milford Haven Fortifications

HAVERFORDWEST

BROAD HAVEN

JOHNSTON

MILFORD HAVEN

FORT SCOVESTON

DALE

NEYLAND

Daugleddau

SAUNDERSFOOT

ANGLE

PEMBROKE DOCK

PEMBROKE

TENBY

PENALLY

MANORBIER

CASTLEMARTIN PENINSULA

0   8 Kms.

0   5 Mls.

FORTS BUILT ABOUT 1580

OTHER EARLY FORTS

MAIN FORTS BUILT 1844-1875

ISLAND FORTS

DEFENSIBLE BARRACKS 1844-45

Map of the main fortifications of the Milford Haven waterway.

north shore of the waterway, and another new town was springing up in conjunction with the naval dockyard not far from Pembroke. Pembroke Dockyard was a natural rail terminus, and plans were afoot for building a railway line from Tenby. North of the Haven there were plans for the creation of a new transatlantic passenger port at Neyland (also known as "New Milford"), connected via Haverfordwest to the South Wales Railway. Suddenly the strategic and commercial importance of Milford Haven was realised by the government, by the railway companies, and also by private developers. And as long as France was a threat to British security, the Haven needed to be defended against maritime attack.

The first large building project was connected with the defence of the Royal Naval Dockyard. The Defensible Barracks, designed to hold a garrison of 500 men, were built between 1844 and 1857. Two martello towers were erected at either end of the Dockyard waterfront. Further down the Haven new forts were constructed between 1850 and 1870 at Dale Fort, Popton Point, Chapel Bay, South Hook Point and Hubberston. In the waterway itself

14

Four of the Milford Haven forts. Above left: South Hook Fort, which is located within the boundary of the Esso Refinery. Above right: Popton Fort, used as the administration centre for the B.P. Angle Bay Ocean Terminal. Below left: the Defensible Barracks at Pembroke Dock. Below right: Thorn Island Fort, used in recent years as an hotel. These forts are all in a good state of repair.

forts were built on Thorn Island and Stack Rock. Plans were also made for the landward defence of the Haven, and a number of sites were selected which could hold off attacks from the south and east. Only two of these additional sites were ever developed — at Fort Scoveston and St.

Catherine's Island, Tenby. Thus by 1870 the Haven was a well-protected waterway, defended by a whole range of strategically located fortifications. The Defensible Barracks held the main defence force, and other large garrisons (of about 200 men) could be housed in the powerful forts at Popton

Point and Hubberston. In all, the Haven forts could accommodate a garrison of about 1900 men, defending the waterway with 220 heavy guns.

During the century or so which has elapsed since the completion of the 19th century forts they have never come under direct attack. Most of the forts are still in good repair, and some are still in use for non-military purposes. For example, Dale Fort is a popular field centre owned by the Field Studies Council, while Popton Point Fort is used as the headquarters of the BP Angle Bay Ocean Terminal.

Left: One of the Pembroke Dock Martello towers.

THE NEW TOWNS

Milford

Milford was the first of the three "new towns" to be built on the shores of the waterway. The town was founded in 1793 on land owned by Sir William Hamilton, and most of its early growth was due to the enthusiasm and energy of his agent Charles Greville. The grid-iron street plan, with three main streets running parallel with the shore, gives the town a morphology quite different from that of the older Pembrokeshire towns. Among the earliest settlers were a group of Quaker whalers from Nantucket. They were enticed by the prospect of an easy market for sperm oil, which was required for lighting the streets of London. After only a few years, however, they abandoned their whaling activities and turned to manufacturing and trading. In the early 1800s, the town prospered with shipbuilding for the Admiralty, fishing, and trade in corn and other local goods. The Navy abandoned the dockyard at Milford in 1814 following a dispute over land purchase, but the small fishing industry was healthy enough, and the town progressed quickly. The Irish steam packet service was based here until 1836, but following its removal to Pembroke Dock there was a period of stagnation, and the population even declined. After many delays Milford Docks were finally completed in 1888, almost a century after the founding of the town.

Lord Nelson Hotel, one of the best-known hotels in Pembrokeshire. The town of Milford is still proud of its links (however tenuous!) with Lord Nelson and Emma Hamilton.

The town developed by fits and starts. After 1888 there were dreams of a great ship-building industry, and it was believed that the town could become a transatlantic passenger terminus. As it happened, the real growth of Milford came largely by accident, resulting from improvements in the design of fishing vessels and the discovery of rich fishing-grounds in the western approaches to the British Isles. Between 1900 and 1914 the proximity of Milford to these fishing-grounds, the excellence of Milford Haven as a port, and the size of Milford Docks themselves led to remarkable growth in the fishing industry. By 1904 there were 66 trawlers and 150 smacks based at the docks, which were used by many other vessels from other ports also. By 1914 about 2,000 local people were employed in the fishing industry, and Milford was in the top league of fishing ports. The large fish market was in constant use. However, the boom could not last and the fortunes of the fishing industry fluctuated violently in the 1920s and 1930s as a result of national economic factors and over-fishing in the western fishing-grounds. The 1939-45 War allowed these fishing-grounds to recover somewhat, and a record

Milford Haven Street Map

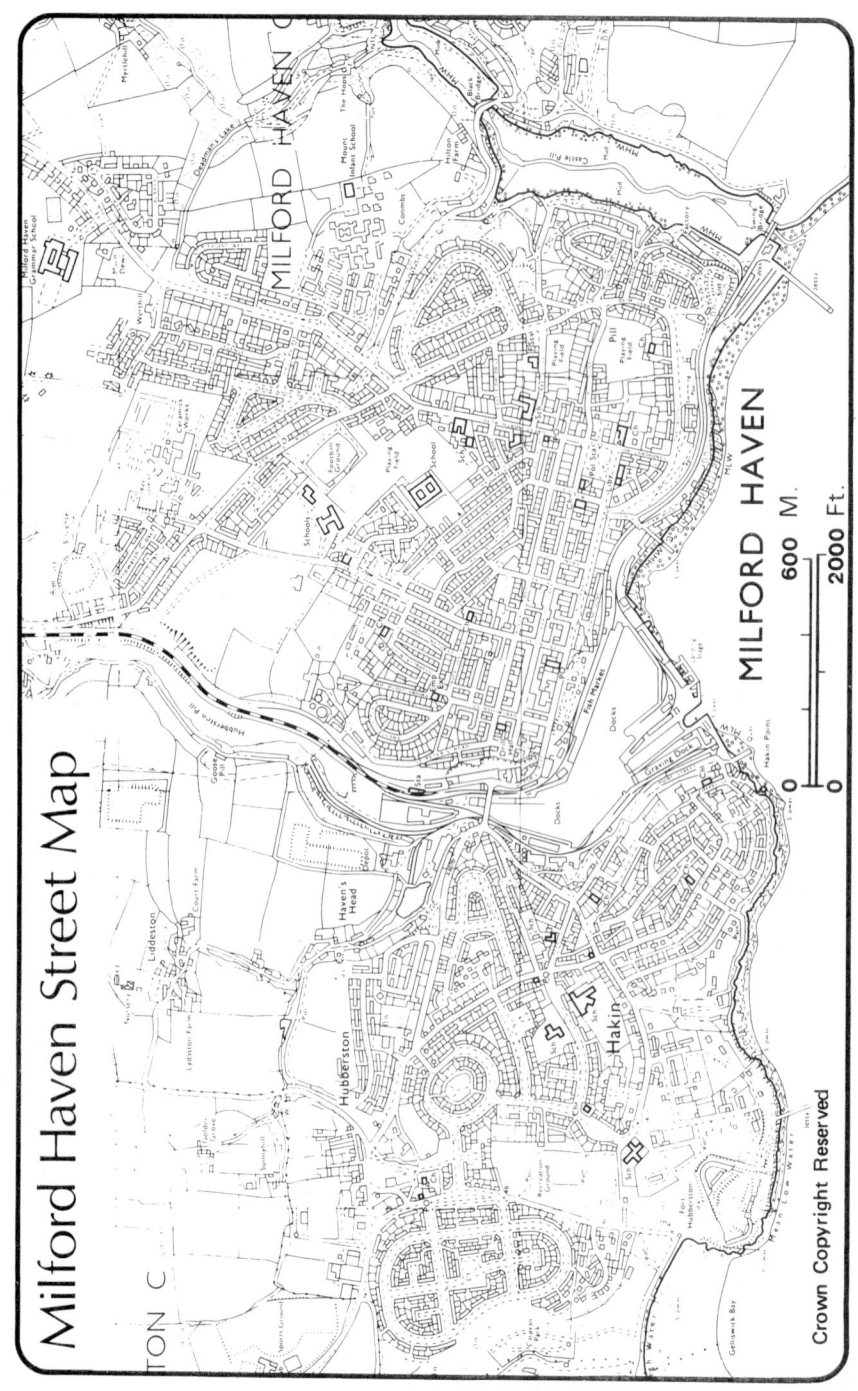

MILFORD HAVEN

600 M.

2000 Ft.

18

catch of 59,286 tons was obtained by the Milford fleet in 1946. As recently as 1950 there were 97 vessels based at the port, including 80 trawlers over 100 ft (30 m) long. In that year the catch was worth £1.6 million, and there were 1,000 men employed on the fishing vessels. But then a slow decline started. Gradually, as catches have become smaller and smaller, the number of trawlers has fallen drastically to a level where the Milford fishing industry seems to be all but dead. Now there are only a handful of vessels and less than 50 full-time fishermen left.

Right: An old photograph of fish barrels being loaded in Milford Docks.

Above: A forest of masts in Milford Docks during the good old days. This photograph was taken shortly after 1900, when the docks were heavily used by trawlers and smacks. Well over 200 vessels were based at the port at this time.

Left: Street map of Milford, showing the Docks, the original town with its grid-iron layout, and the large areas of modern housing with curved streets in the eastern part of the town and in the suburbs of Hakin and Hubberston.

19

Neyland

Further up the waterway, near the northern end of the Haven Bridge, lies the small town of Neyland. Like Milford, it was a planned settlement, although it was built much later. It was designed by Brunel, during the "railway era" of the mid-nineteenth century. He chose the site (previously a small fishing-port) as the terminus for the South Wales Railway, intending that passenger trains should connect with the Atlantic passenger service and the Irish Packet Service. The railway line was completed to the port of 'New Milford' in 1856. The town was planned with a grid-iron layout, and for a decade or so there was much building activity. Neyland enjoyed a brief period of prosperity. A wagon-works was established at the railway terminus, providing much local employment. There was a small shipyard. The fishing industry boomed, and a refrigeration factory was built to provide ice for the rapid transport of fish to the South Wales fish markets.

Neyland never became a great transatlantic port. Comparatively little Atlantic shipping could be induced to call, for there was no deep-water frontage. In 1906 even the Irish Service was transferred to Fishguard. There was competition, too, from the other town of Milford Haven which had greater "growth potential". On the opposite shore of the Haven Pembroke Dock acquired its railway link in 1864 and was rapidly developed as a Naval Dockyard, and by 1863 Milford had its own railway line as well. These developments meant that Neyland's advantages were much reduced, particularly since the Admiralty would not allow developments which might congest the upper reaches of the Haven. The little town declined gradually, losing its fishing industry and its ice-factory, its shipyard and its wagon-works. Although the rail depot kept some wagon-repairing facilities until the post-war era, these closed down with the rail service in 1955. In 1971 the track was lifted. Until 1974 there was a car ferry service between Neyland and Hobbs Point; but this stopped running when the Haven Bridge was opened, allowing the constant flow of traffic between the two shores of the Haven to by-pass the town completely.

The "Cleddau King", a vehicle and passenger ferry which plied between Neyland and Hobbs Point until the opening of the Haven Bridge in 1974. This photograph was taken in 1970.

Pembroke Dock

Pembroke Dock thrived on the early failures of the other new towns of Milford Haven, and it is the only town in Pembrokeshire ever to have acquired a real 'industrial' image. Its early growth occurred after 1814, when Paterchurch was selected as the site for the new Admiralty dockyard. The site was sheltered and spacious, and there was deep water close inshore. There was a long tradition of local ship-building and a pool of skilled labour. Moreover, the Haven was remote enough from the troubles of the European mainland to serve as a strategically 'safe' base for major technological developments in naval shipbuilding. For this was indeed an exciting time; there were experiments with steam propulsion, with paddles and with screw propellers, and with iron cladding. Warships were increasing rapidly in

size. Once established, the Dockyard was the scene of many innovations in shipbuilding, and it is not often realised that for most of the century Pembroke Dock was the most advanced shipbuilding yard in the world. The year 1834 saw the launching of *Tartarus,* the Dockyard's first steam man-of-war; in 1846 *Conflict* was launched, being the yard's first warship fitted with a screw propeller; and 1847 saw the launching of the Lion, then the largest warship in the Royal Navy. In 1852 the *Duke of Wellington,* the largest three-decker in the world, was completed. The shipyard produced five royal yachts, and there was a long line of Naval barques, brigantines, cruisers, gunboats and battleships. In 1875 the Chief Constructor of the American Navy referred to the Dockyard as the finest shipbuilding yard in the world. In

The launch of the Royal Yacht "Victoria and Albert" at the Royal Dockyard in 1855. This is a contemporary engraving.

Pembroke Dock Street Map

ST. MARY CP

PEMBROKE DOCK

PEMBROKE

0   500 M.

0   1500 Ft.

Crown Copyright Reserved

Left: Street plan of Pembroke Dock, showing the grid-iron street layout, the Dockyard, the Defensible Barracks and the two oil storage depots at Llanreath and Llanion..

all, the Dockyard saw the construction of more than 250 naval vessels, and at its height in the later years of the nineteenth century it employed over 3,000 men. Many employees travelled daily to work by rowing-boat from other parts of the Haven.

In the early years of the present century Pembroke Dock was still one of the main industrial centres of West Wales, and during the First World War the Dockyard worked at full pace, specialising in the building of small, swift cruisers. But its remoteness was beginning to count as a disadvantage, and in 1926 it was abruptly closed. The town was thrown into despair. The whole community suffered a great deal of hardship, and the bitter memories of this time have still not entirely disappeared. Hundreds of families left the area, and the unemployment rate approached 25 per cent.

During the Second World War the town became one of the major flying-boat bases, and part of the Dockyard was again used as a naval base for ship-repairing. Innumerable Atlantic convoys in the dark years of the War were assembled here in the sheltered waters of the Haven, and minelaying, minesweeping and escort work was co-ordinated from the Milford Haven H.Q. It has been estimated that during the course of the war some 12,000 cargo vessels and 5,000 warships sailed from the Haven. The town became an important fuel storage depot, and there was a sizeable garrison. But these wartime activities were a mixed

blessing, for the town attracted enemy bombing attacks and suffered greatly from air-raids. There was considerable destruction and loss of life in the town, particularly during the twelve months between July 1940 and June 1941. The main enemy targets were the oil storage tanks at Llanreath, the Llanion Barracks, and the Dockyard.

The town continued to be used as a base for the Sunderland flying-boats of R.A.F. Coastal Command until 1957 and the Navy still maintains a small presence at Pembroke Dock. Since the 1950s very little use has been made of the Dockyard, although part of it has been used by small private shipbuilding and ship-repairing concerns, and within the last decade one section has been a shore base for Celtic Sea oil exploration work. Several factories have been built within the last 30 years on the outskirts of the town in an attempt to solve the chronic unemployment problem, but unfortunately these factories have had a history made up of more failures than successes.

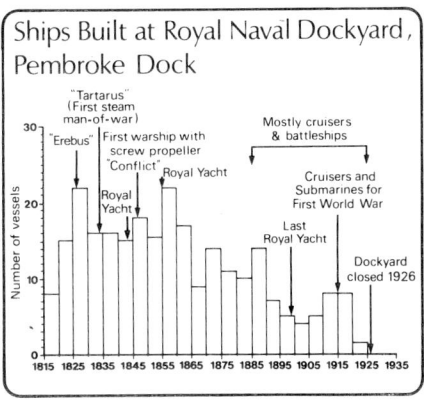

The rise and decline of the Pembroke Dock ship-building industry. The Royal Dockyard closed in 1926.

THE OIL INDUSTRY

During the early 1950s the oil companies were beginning to plan for the widespread use of supertankers or VLCCs[1]. As they did so, they recognised the immense advantages of Milford Haven as a potential oil port. Its wide, sheltered waterway could accommodate vessels of 56 ft (17 m) draught at all states of the tide. Tidal scour was efficient, and there was no silting problem. Land was cheap and available for large-scale construction projects. Moreover, the Government favoured the development of the Haven. Consequently the decision was taken in 1957-58 to embark upon the creation of a major oil port.

The Esso Refinery, near the village of Herbrandston, was the first oil refinery to be built on the shores of Milford Haven. It began working in 1960 and is now the second largest refinery in the British Isles, able to refine 15 million tons of oil per year. The refinery's land covers 710 acres (287 ha). The Esso jetty, stretching about 3,000 ft (900 m) out from the shore, is used by tankers of all sizes up to 285,000 tons, and nowadays more than 1,200 vessels use the jetty each year.

The B.P. Ocean Terminal, at Popton Point, near Angle, was officially opened in 1961. Its cost was approximately £7 million. The B.P. Company holds 383 acres (154 ha) of land on the south shore of Milford Haven, of which less than 300 acres is currently used. The offices and control centre for the terminal are inside the old Popton Fort, but the main tank farm is over a mile away at Kilpaison, on the shore of Angle Bay. These tanks hold a total of half a million tons of crude oil. The jetty at Popton Point provides three berths for VLCCs of up to 250,000 tons. There is no B.P. refinery on the site. Instead, the terminal was built to import and store crude oil for the existing B.P. refinery at Llandarcy, near Swansea Docks, which could not handle VLCCs. The terminal and the refinery are connected by a buried pipe-line over 62 miles (100 km) long which can carry 9.2 million tons of oil per year.

The No. 2 berthing head of jetty at BP's Angle Bay Ocean Terminal.

---

[1] VLCC stands for Very Large Crude Carrier.

The BP Ocean Terminal at Popton Point. The tanker is the 215,000 ton "British Explorer". The offices and control centre for the terminal are located in the old Popton Fort.

The Texaco Refinery near Pembroke was the company's first U.K. refining plant. It was opened in October 1964, and it is the only refinery on the south shore of the Haven. The tank farm and refinery are built in the middle of the 925 acre (373 ha) site, near the small village of Rhoscrowther. Since it was built the refinery has been enlarged so that it can now refine about 10 million tons of crude oil per year. The Texaco jetty can accommodate tankers of more than 250,000 tons. About 70 per cent of refined products are shipped out, for road access to the refinery is poor and there is no rail link. A recent development at the Texaco site is the construction of a £290 million "cat cracker" for the Pembroke Cracking Company. This new company, financed by both Gulf and Texaco, will greatly increase the local production of petrol for both companies.

The Gulf Oil Refinery, together with its petrochemical plant and marine terminal was formally opened by the Queen in August 1968. The refinery and its tank farm are built on an exposed plateau site overlooking the inner reaches of the waterway. The three berths of the jetty project only a short distance from the shore, where they are adjacent to the main channel. However, because the water here is not so deep as it is in the outer part of the Haven the largest vessels which can be handled at present are 165,000-tonners. Until recently the company had an importing strategy which involved the use of a deep-water terminal on Bantry Bay in Eire. 'Mammoth' tankers of 325,000 tons called at Bantry Bay with cargoes of crude oil, and after storage in a tank farm this oil was trans-shipped in smaller tankers to the Gulf refineries at Waterston and

Europoort (Holland). Since the terrible accident which destroyed the Bantry Bay terminal in 1979 the company has had to re-think its strategy, and now most of the oil for the Milford Haven refinery is imported direct. At present the refinery can process about five million tons of crude oil per year. Some of the products are used on the site in Gulf's petrochemical plant, which is the only one in the Milford Haven area. The plant produces benzene and cyclohexene, needed in the manufacture of nylon. There are other products also, shipped partly to the Rotterdam chemical industry and partly to other European customers.

The £30 million **Amoco Refinery** came 'on stream' in October 1973, with a refining capacity of four million tons per year. In 1975 this capacity was increased, and it has recently been increased again through the building of a new "cat-cracker" unit costing £85 million. Unlike the other Milford Haven refineries the Amoco site lies well away from the coast. It does, however, have its own jetty a short distance east of the Esso Terminal, and it can handle 275,000-tonners. Underground pipelines connect the jetty to the refinery. The refinery at present occupies only about one-eighth of the 1936 acres (782 ha) owned by Amoco.

Pembroke Power Station, which is located on the south shore of the Haven, is one of the largest in Europe. It was completed in 1975 at a cost of £105 million. The power station burns about four million tons of oil per year; this is carried from the Gulf and Texaco refineries and the B.P. Ocean Terminal by buried pipelines. Output is 2,000 megawatts, carried by 400 kV supergrid power-lines across South Wales

Pembroke Power Station, one of the largest oil-fired power stations in Europe. It produces 2,000 megawatts of electricity.

towards the Midlands and the Bristol region. The power station provides employment for 495 people, and it contributes over £2 million to the local economy each year in rates and indirect contributions.

Of the vast network of pipelines which are essential to the workings of the Milford Haven oil refining complex, the most important is the **'3M's' pipeline** linking Milford Haven with the Midlands and Manchester. It carries a variety of refined products (mainly petrol, kerosene and diesel fuel) to Seisdon in Staffordshire. From Seisdon there are smaller pipelines to terminals in Birmingham, Nottingham and Manchester. The main pipeline is theoretically capable of carrying over nine million tons of petroleum products each year, although it is currently operating at only 60 per cent of capacity.

The Milford Haven oil industry has grown at a spectacular rate. From small beginnings the Haven had become by 1968 Britain's leading oil port, handling 30 million tons out of a U.K. total of 180 million tons. Now the Haven handles the largest volume of cargo in Britain. In 1974 (the peak year) over 33 million tons of shipping used the port. There were over 10,000 ship movements, and the cargo handled (mostly crude oil and petroleum products) was over 59 million tons. Vessels of over 300,000 tons are now using the waterway, and cargoes of 225,000 tons are commonplace.

Right: One of the Conservancy Board pilot launches operating in the Milford Haven waterway.

The Conservancy Board

The impact of the oil industry in and around Milford Haven has been very great indeed. The most important of the "ancilliaries" is the Milford Haven Conservancy Board, the harbour authority responsible for controlling shipping operations in the waterway. It was set up as a unique civil port authority by Act of Parliament in 1958. It was charged with maintaining and improving the navigation of the whole tidal area of Milford Haven, regulating seaborne traffic, and providing lights, buoys and communications. Also, it was given the right to levy dues on all vessels entering the Haven, in order to finance its operations.

The Conservancy Board is based at Hubberston Point, a location which provides good access to all the refinery jetties and to the harbour entrance. The day-to-day running of its operations is in the hands of a General Manager and a

Harbourmaster. The Board uses the services of 22 self-employed pilots, and it operates five diesel-engined launches for pilotage and other services to ships.

The biggest project undertaken by the Conservancy Board to date was the £7½ million rock dredging scheme of 1967-70, designed to improve the deep-water channel so that it could be safely used by 275,000 ton tankers at all states of the tide. New day and night transit lights were put up to supplement the existing navigational lights. Another large project was undertaken in 1978-1979, when the Board constructed a £6½ million all-tidal ferry terminal for the B & I ferry services to the south coast of Ireland. The commencement of this service, to Cork and Rosslare, brought back to the Haven the "Irish Connection" which left Neyland on the opposite shore 75 years ago.

Exploration in the Celtic Sea

Studies of the Celtic Sea and St. George's Channel have shown geologists that there are probably reserves of crude oil and natural gas deep beneath the sea bed. These will not be as large as those of the North Sea, but in the present energy crisis both the government and the oil companies are keen to discover and exploit all possible offshore oilfields. Drilling for oil and natural gas commenced in the Celtic Sea in 1973, and by mid-1974 natural gas had already been discovered in the Irish sector.

Milford Haven is well placed for taking part in the Celtic Sea oil search. It has its own oil industry and Milford Docks and Pembroke Dockyard are sites which can be used as shore bases. In the initial period of oil exploration (1973-1977) some local companies were involved in providing ship-building and repair and storage facilities. The vast number of services required for drilling operations in the difficult waters off the Dyfed coast encouraged many smaller firms to commit themselves to the Celtic Sea oil search. Near Haverfordwest the runways of Withybush aerodrome were resurfaced, and were used frequently by air taxi and helicopter services. Another helicopter base was in use at Pembroke Dock.

In 1977 the first phase of the oil search, which had involved the drilling of only eight wells, came to an end. This was partly because the oil exploration companies were fully committed in the North Sea and partly because of the world shortage of deep-sea drilling equipment. Also, the oil companies seem to have been disappointed by their initial discoveries in the Celtic Sea; as far as we know crude oil has still not been found off the Pembrokeshire coast.

Drilling activity on board the drill-ship "Havdrill", on station in the Celtic Sea in 1974.

MILFORD HAVEN TODAY

At the present time the character of the Milford Haven waterway is dominated by the oil industry. The industry has brought undoubted wealth to the area, but it would be foolish to pretend that the environment has not suffered. The presence of the National Park was not enough to prevent the development of the outer and middle reaches of the waterway; in spite of the strong objections of the National Parks Commission and the National Park Committee a number of oil installations have been permitted "in the national interest" within the National Park boundary. The B.P. terminal and tank farm are located entirely within the Park and the Esso, Amoco and Texaco refineries straddle its boundary. In and around Milford Haven it is impossible to escape from the visual impact of refineries, tank farms, supertankers, jetties and navigational aids. The huge 700 ft (213 m) Pembroke Power Station chimney stack is now matched by the tall stacks of the refineries which have been built during the expansion projects of the last few years. To the south of the waterway the double row of electricity pylons carrying 400 kV towards Swansea makes a huge impact upon the gently undulating landscape.

Plumes of smoke and towering condensation clouds are now to be seen in the skies above Milford Haven, and in certain weather conditions the smell of oil and smoke hangs heavy in the air. At full production the Pembroke Power Station ejects 650 tons of poisonous sulphur dioxide into the atmosphere every day, and another 350 tons per day is added by the oil refineries. Air pollution is, not surprisingly, a source of great local concern in the Milford Haven towns. Oil pollution in the waterway is less of a problem; stringent safety controls by the Conservancy Board, and very stiff fines imposed by magistrates on tanker captains responsible for oil spills, have ensured that Milford Haven is the cleanest oil port in the world.

At the present time the people of Milford Haven and the surrounding area depend less than one might expect upon the oil industry for their livelihood. Although many local men have found employment on refinery building and expansion projects, the direct employment created by the industry is not great, with under 1,500 jobs in the refineries themselves. However, there are another 1,500 jobs in the port, in the CEGB Power Station, and in the ancillary activities

The tank farm and refinery stacks on the Esso site.

needed to keep the refineries working efficiently. Many jobs are provided in farming, which is still the staple activity in the rich agricultural districts around the waterway. Dairy farming is the main activity, but many farms close to the shores of the Haven are involved in growing early potatoes and also high-value crops such as broccoli and cauliflowers. Jobs in light manufacturing are provided at Milford Haven and Pembroke Dock, but local unemployment rates remain at a worrying level; the rundown of the Milford fishing industry, the standstill in the Celtic Sea oil search, and the

Below: Milford Haven's High Level Bridge after its collapse in June 1970. This caused a prolonged delay before the Bridge was opened to traffic in 1975, finally allowing road traffic to pass unimpeded between the north and south shores of the waterway.

failure of local shipbuilding operations at Pembroke Dock have all added people to the lengthening dole queues.

Tourism has become an important activity in and around Milford Haven, in spite of the massive presence of the oil industry. There is no doubt that the huge super-tankers which visit the waterway are tourist attractions

Above: Sailing boat on the waters of Milford Haven.

Below: Tourist pressure on car-parking facilities at West Angle.

drawing people to the town of Milford and to other vantage points such as St. Ann's Head and West Angle Bay. Boat trips from Hobbs Point and Milford Haven itself provide a good way of seeing the waterway and its oil installations, and the CEGB has a programme of guided tours in which holiday-makers can look over the Pembroke Power Station. On the outer shores of the Haven, Dale, Angle and West Angle are popular holiday centres, and there is a holiday camp near Pembroke Dock. Beaches such as Sandy Haven, Lindsway Bay and Watwick Bay are becoming increasingly popular.

Inevitably, waterbourne recreation is the greatest of Milford Haven's attractions. The waterway as a whole (including the Dangleddau section) has moorings for over 1,000 pleasure craft, and there are sailing clubs and dinghy parks at Dale, Gelliswick Bay, Neyland and Pembroke Dock. Sailing races and regattas are held in the waterway during the summer, and power-boat racing is the latest thing at Hazelbeach, Burton, Dale and Gelliswick. Sea-angling is a popular sport based at Milford, and of course

Two freezer trawlers and a smaller Milford Haven trawler alongside the fish quay of Milford Docks. Freezer trawlers and reefer ships have been using the Docks as a base in recent years.

there are keen fishermen along all the shores of the waterway.

The future of Milford Haven is to a large extent tied to the future of the energy supply industry in Britain. Already the oil industry contributes hugely to the local economy in the form of rates. Large expansion schemes (and diversification of products) at the Texaco, Gulf and Amoco refineries guarantee that the oil industry will maintain its presence here at least until the end of the century, and if the Celtic Sea oil search gets under way again many local businesses will profit. The future of Milford Docks still looks insecure. The facilities there are now widely used by Hull freezer trawlers and for the trans-shipment of Mackerel and other catches from fishing vessels to reefer ships, which export the fish to tropical countries. On the other hand the perennial problems of over-fishing and fishing quota impositions makes it difficult to predict the future. The B & I passenger service between Pembroke Dock and the south coast of Ireland is bringing a much-needed boost to the dockyard town, and there are now elaborate plans for the construction of a "super-dock" on the waterfront at Milford. The Milford "super-dock" will, if it is ever built, bring undoubted benefits to the town's economy; but the prospect of a large industrial site along the sea front has brought a great deal of local opposition on amenity grounds. In spite of the delays, disasters, frustrations and false alarms which have punctuated the history of Milford Haven, it still remains a place of high hopes and great aspirations.